Sekiya Miyoshi

JONAH
AND THE
BIG FISH

THE
PILGRIM
PRESS
Cleveland

Long ago lived a giant fish who glowed like all the colors
of the rainbow. This fish played in the deep blue sea.
Sometimes it came up to where the air and water meet.
One such day, it saw a young man sleeping on top of the cliffs.

The fish saw the young man, Jonah, wake up with a start.
While asleep, Jonah had heard a voice call his name.
"Jonah, go at once to Nineveh, that great city, and cry out
against it; for their wickedness has come up before me."
Jonah awoke, raised his head, and looked all around.
He did not see the fish; he did not see God.
He saw only his donkey.

Then Jonah wondered, "Has God spoken to me? But this trip doesn't make any sense. Nineveh is so far away from here, even with my donkey. The people there are very bad; even God has seen this. And what good can I do there? I am only one small person."

Did Jonah want to go to Nineveh? No, but he was afraid to just stay home. So Jonah had an idea. "What if I go on a trip, but to some other place?"

Secretly he left his house, his land, and his donkey—and fled from God.

Jonah walked a long time. Finally he came to Joppa, the seaport.
Quietly Jonah boarded a ship where he hoped God would not find him.

Jonah's plan was clever. This ship was sailing to Tarshish,
at the end of the sea.
The water was deep blue, and the sky was calm.
Jonah felt safe aboard the ship. He was tired from all his walking,
and he fell asleep.

All this time, the big fish had followed.

Suddenly a strong wind roared across the sea. The ship tipped one way, then the other. The storm was so mighty that the ship threatened to break up.

The sailors were afraid, and everyone cried to their gods, "Save us! Save us!" But the storm grew stronger. The sailors then threw the cargo into the sea, to make the ship lighter.

But Jonah had gone below the deck, laid down, and was fast asleep. The captain came to him and said, "What are you doing sound asleep? Get up and call on your god! Perhaps your god will spare us a thought so that we do not sink with our ship."

Jonah awoke and knew what was happening. "I wanted to hide from God who made the seas and the dry land. This storm is because I am running away. Toss me into the sea, and it will be calm again."

So the sailors prayed to God and tossed Jonah overboard into the wild sea.

And the sea ceased from its raging.

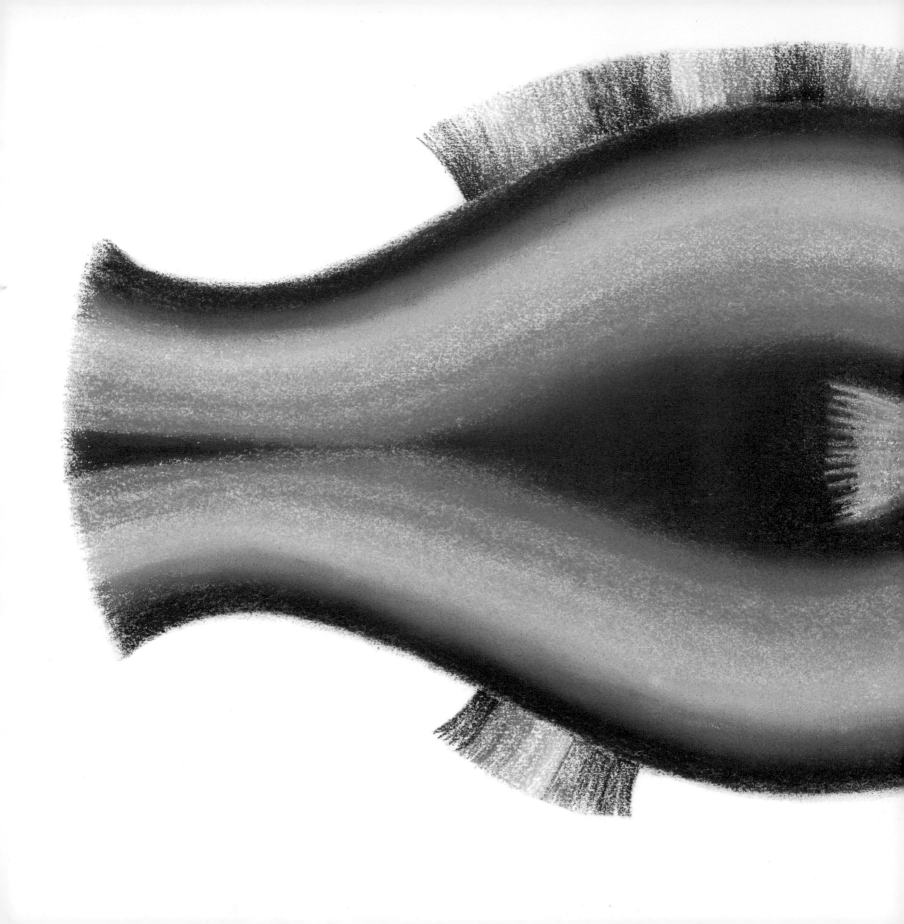

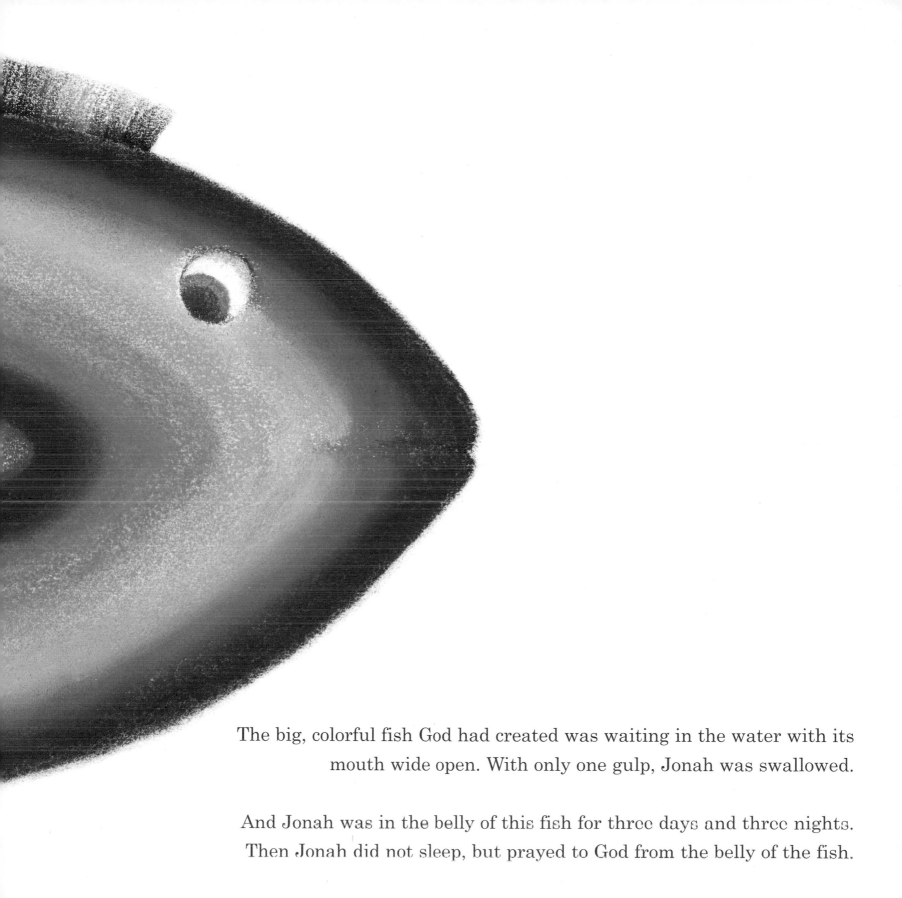

The big, colorful fish God had created was waiting in the water with its mouth wide open. With only one gulp, Jonah was swallowed.

And Jonah was in the belly of this fish for three days and three nights. Then Jonah did not sleep, but prayed to God from the belly of the fish.

When the time was right, God spoke to the colorful fish, and it spit
Jonah out. He flew into the air and landed with a plop on the dry
land. He filled his lungs with fresh air instead of fishy air.
He sat outside in the sunshine instead of inside a sloppy wet fish.
Then God nudged him again. "Jonah, get up and go to Nineveh."

But could it be? The city of Nineveh was close by!

This time Jonah traveled according to God's direction.

Nineveh was a large city! A person would need three days to walk from one side to the other.

Jonah decided to walk just one day into the city and called with a loud voice, "In forty days, Ninevah shall be destroyed!"

Then Jonah quickly ran off and climbed to the top of a hill.

He was afraid that the bad people of Nineveh would hurt him.

But the people of Nineveh who had heard Jonah became fearful. They were sorry about their evil doings.

Even the king took off his robe, put on ragged clothes, and sat in ashes.

He proclaimed that no one—not even animals or pets—should eat food or drink water.

Instead everyone must be friendly with one another. And everyone prayed to God day after day, asking for God's forgiveness.

Because of these changes, God decided to protect the city and not let it be destroyed.

Jonah didn't know about this change. He had run to the top of the hill so that he could see the city of Nineveh destroyed.

In the burning sun he watched patiently—and waited for its destruction.
But nothing happened. The city was now safe as people did not harm each other.

God had forgiven the people of Nineveh.

But Jonah had not forgiven them. He had been awakened at his home, nearly drowned in a storm, lived in the belly of a big fish, and come all this way to Ninevah. God's promises are always kept. "So let the destruction begin," Jonah prayed to God.

While Jonah sat there waiting for something to happen, a tall bush started to grow behind him. Its branches got so large and heavy with leaves that the sun's heat was blocked out. Jonah was grateful for the shade that day. He thought that tomorrow would be even cooler under the bush's branches.

The next morning, however, a worm chewed off all the leaves from the bush. Only a few small leaves remained. When the sun rose, Jonah was standing in the burning heat again. Even the breeze was hotter today than yesterday. And he became very angry.

God had sent him to Nineveh to announce its destruction. Yet the city remained unharmed. Yesterday the bush grew and gave him shade. But today it was without leaves, and the sun burned him again.

Oh, Jonah was hot with anger.

Then Jonah heard God's voice for the third time.

"Why are you angry, Jonah? You feel sorry for the bush, but you did not even plant it yourself. Should I not feel sorry for the people of the big city of Nineveh, whom I have created? They have asked for forgiveness, and I have forgiven them."

Then Jonah was no longer angry.

God cares for the colorful fish, the bush, and Ninevah. God cares about all animals, plants, and people.

What happened after this the Bible does not say. But Jonah went home, no doubt, to take care of his donkey. He probably worked every day and lived happily with his family. Jonah probably told them many times about his great trip to Ninevah. They knew that God's care also included them.

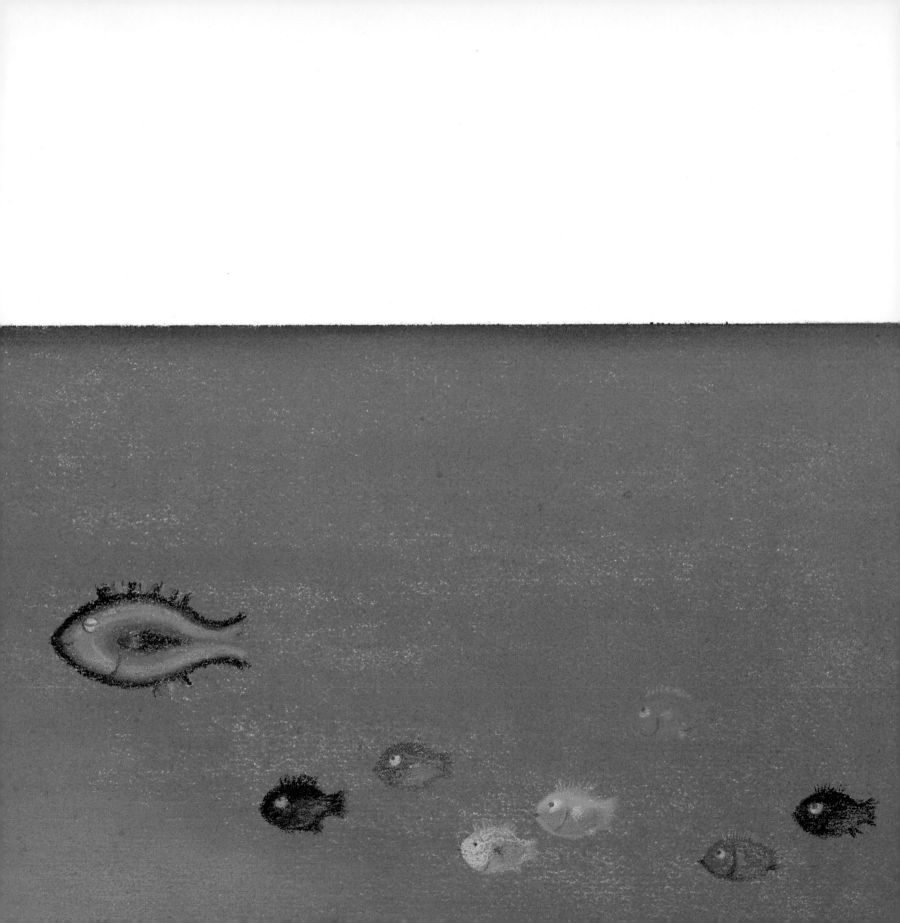

And what about the big, colorful fish? No doubt this fish had many children and grandchildren. And they all glowed with the colors of the rainbow.

The fish reminds us today of Jonah and his useless running away. God used the big, colorful fish to land Jonah on the beach near Nineveh. Jonah discovered that God cares for plants, animals, and peoples of every land.

JONAH AND THE BIG FISH

English text copyright © 2002 by The Pilgrim Press
700 Prospect Avenue
Cleveland, Ohio 44115-1100 U.S.A.
pilgrimpress.com

Illustration and Original Text © Hisae Miyoshi
Original Japanese Edition "Yonato ookina sakana"
published in 1977 by Shiko-Sha Co., Ltd., Tokyo, Japan
Printed in China
07 06 05 04 03 02   5 4 3 2 1
ISBN 0-8298-1511-2